Abraham Leggett

The narrative of Major Abraham Leggett of the army of the revolution

Now first printed from the original manuscript

Abraham Leggett

The narrative of Major Abraham Leggett of the army of the revolution

Now first printed from the original manuscript

ISBN/EAN: 9783337235123

Printed in Europe, USA, Canada, Australia, Japan

Cover: Foto ©ninafisch / pixelio.de

More available books at **www.hansebooks.com**

MAJ. ABRAHAM LEGGETT.

THE

NARRATIVE

OF

MAJOR ABRAHAM LEGGETT,

OF THE ARMY OF THE REVOLUTION.

Now first Printed from the Original Manuscript.

WRITTEN BY HIMSELF.

WITH

AN INTRODUCTION AND NOTES,

BY

CHARLES I. BUSHNELL.

NEW YORK:
PRIVATELY PRINTED
1865.

To

ABRAHAM ALSOP LEGGETT,

(Eldest Son of Major Leggett),

This Work,

AS A TOKEN OF ESTEEM AND FRIENDSHIP,

IS

RESPECTFULLY INSCRIBED.

INTRODUCTION.

MAJOR ABRAHAM LEGGETT, the author of the following narrative, was the son of John Leggett, by his wife Sarah, and was born in the town of West Farms, Westchester County, N. Y., on the third day of January, 1755.

When about seven years of age he lost his father, and was placed under the care of his grandfather, William Leggett, with whom he remained until the death of that gentleman, when he was taken under the care of his uncle, Abraham Leggett. He continued with him until he had reached his fourteenth year, when he was apprenticed to Phineas

Hunt, and subsequently to Samuel Van Black, to learn the trade of a blacksmith. His opportunities for education were, therefore, but very limited, his early years being devoted to the toils of a trade, and occasionally to the labors of a farm.

When the troubles with the mother country assumed the proportions of civil war, our author took a decided and active part in support of the rights of the colonists, rendering to his country some important services, and distinguishing himself in the contest by his courage and patriotism. He was engaged in the battle of Brooklyn, where he behaved with gallantry, and he took an important part in covering the retreat of the American army from Long Island, being one of the last to leave the shore.

He was afterwards engaged in the action at Harlem Heights, and in the battle of White Plains. Subsequently he was ordered to Fort Montgomery, on the Hudson, and when that post, after a stout and bloody resistance, fell into the hands of the British, he became a prisoner of war, and was confined in the Old City Hall in Wall-street, and

OLD CITY HALL.

Wall St. N. Y.

afterwards in the Old Provost in the Park, where he suffered at the hands of the enemy the greatest privation and cruelty.

Our author remained a prisoner until the year 1781, when his liberation was effected by exchange. He subsequently rejoined the army, and was engaged in various skirmishes and expeditions, chiefly in New Jersey and on Long Island. He remained thus engaged until near the termination of the war, discharging his duties with zeal and ability, gaining the respect and esteem of his comrades, and retiring from the service with the character of a fearless soldier, a spotless patriot, and an upright, honest man.

At the termination of the war, he opened a crockery store in Peck Slip, N. Y.; afterwards went to Charleston, S. C.; subsequently moved to Georgia, and then returned to New York. Here he became engaged for a while in the dry goods business as a member of the house of Leggett, Drake & Co., and then went into the blacksmith's business, under a contract with the Government of the United States. He subsequently moved to Illinois, where he remained for two or three years, returning to New York about the year 1822, after which time he did but little business.

Major Leggett was twice married: first to Rebecca, daughter of John Morgan, of Huntington, L. I. By her he had two children. She died at North Salem, in Westchester County, N. Y., on the twelfth day of June, 1780. His second wife was Catharine Wiley, of New Rochelle, who died in the city of New York on the twenty-ninth day of November, in the year 1839. By this lady he had nine children, among which was William Leggett, so well known as an able writer, and as the editor at one time of the "New York Evening Post," a paper which then held, and still retains, for editorial ability, the foremost rank among the press of our city.

In his personal appearance, our author was about five feet eight inches in stature, and rather stout. His eyes were of a hazel color, and his hair originally dark. He had a fine, full, open countenance, kind and benevolent in expression. In his bearing, he was dignified but cordial, and his manners were

THE OLD DUTCH CHURCH, BROOKLYN, N. Y.

affable and pleasing. In his religious belief, he was a Presbyterian, and, for the last few years of his life, a member of the Dutch Reformed Church. He was an original member of the New-York State Society of the Cincinnati, having been admitted at its organization, and in the year 1838 was elected its Vice-President, which office he held at the time of his death. He died, after a short illness, at the residence of his son, Abraham A. Leggett, in the city of New York, on the sixteenth day of January, 1842, in the eighty-eighth year of his age. His remains, followed by a large concourse of sincere mourners, were conveyed to the Presbyterian burying-ground in Houston-street, where they were interred with every mark of honor and respect.

At the request of his children, Major Leggett, in the latter part of his life, commenced writing out a narrative of his revolutionary services. This, however, he did not live to complete. The part which is extant, and which we here present to the reader, though faulty in orthography, the result of his defective education, is nevertheless worthy of preservation. As a narrative of a sufferer in the British prisons in our city, it is not only interesting but valuable, and it is equally so as the record of one who was not only a cotemporary, but a prominent actor in the memorable struggles of the "times that tried men's souls."

NARRATIVE.

I WAS born Jan'y 3d, 1755. My farther John, (1) the son of William Joined A Company of Volenteers and march'd for Canaday in the year 1759—they Proceded as far as Lake George and there he was Taken with the Fever and died within four days, in the year 1762—my mother left West farms and moved to Newtown, Long Island, with four Children—one sister older than myself and Two yonger and a yonger Brother. My Grand Farther Capt. William Leggett had a desire to have me left with him. I at this Time was about Seven years of age—my Grand Farther died in 1764 or 65—I then Remaned with my uncle Abraham till I was 14 years old. I was then Put apprentice To Phenas Hunt, Blacksmith—there I had but a Poor opertunity to Get the Trade for I was Put to the Farming more than Shop. I grew dissatisfide and aplyde to my Gardian my uncle A, that I had no Prospect for larning the Trade being kept mostly on the farm. In July my Indenture was Given up after Serving him three years for my vittels and a Very scant Supply of Clothes; In August I Came to New York and Put myself apprentice to Sam'l Van Black, Black Smith—this was in the year 1772. I was then at the Jany following 18, and agreed to stay with him four years, but in '75 the Troubles with England commenced, and nothing to be done, and I had an oppertunity to Get in Public service. I agreed to Go on to Pokipsey and do work on the Two Frigates (2) that was to be Built there by order of the Continal Congress then sitting In Philadelphia on the first of Febru'ry 1776 several that was Engaged and walk'd to Pokipsey 83 miles—there I was Engadg'd Till the first July. I then with several others Formed ourselves in a company under the command of Barnardus Swartout (3) all Vollenteers—the Times began to appear Very Interesting—the British Fleet and large army was at Statten Island (4)—we march'd off In High Spirrits Till we

Got to the Calder-barrack near the Croton River—there we Staid but three Days for Derection—we then had news that English army was Preparing to land on Long Island (5)—that they Easy affected under The Protection of Shiping—our army was at this Time on Brooklin Hights* fortifying as fast as they Could—the Enemy advanced upon Part of our army under the com'd of Lord Sterling (6) and General Sullivan (7)—they Faught on the Retreat to flat Bush Hills. (8) There the battle became Very Hot but the Enemy was too Powerful—they extended there write wing so as to Cut off the Retreat of our detachment from the main army which they succeeded in and they kill'd and Captured many, amongst them was several officers and the Two Gen'ls—many was Drownded in the mill Pond. (9) This took Place 28th august 1776 (10)—the next day the 29, Capt. Swartout crowsed with us to the Island and we was Placed on the Left from the Hill call'd Fort Green (11) to Wallabout—the Two armies close in View of Each other, and for three Days the Rain fell in Torrents so that we could not Cook—then was the first Time I was Brought to Eat Raw Pork—the last night we was on the Island myself and Several of Volunteers was Put on advanced Centres with speshel orders How to behave Should we discover

* A battery of eight guns was constructed here.

the Enemy advancing—the night was Foggy & Very Dark. Some Circumstance made all the Centres Return on the lines but myself—my Remaning at my Station was Imputed to Bravery. Early in the morning yet Very Dark we was Paraded under the Report that we was to attack the Enemy in there lines we was Led around we new not where till I Saw the old Stone Church of Brooklin (12)—then an officer Riding by Says, a Groce mistake—we was orded to wheel about and Reman the lines, wich we did—a dangerous attempt—there we Remaned Till Some Time after—we then formed the Rear Gard we was orderd forward, Still expected to meet the Enemy Till we found ourselves at the Ferry and the army all cross'd (13) But the Gard then under the Command of Gen'l Mifflin (14)—we then was order'd to Choak up the Street with waggons and Carts to Prevent the Light Horse from Rushing Down upon us—at this time no boats—I Prepar'd myself to Swim the River flood tide But Fortunately Two Battoes Struck the Shore—by this Time there was but a Few of us left—we all Hurred on Board and Shoved off—the Enemy Rush'd Down on the Hill and Commenced a Brisk fire. Fortunately no one was Hurt in our Boat—the other Boat had four wounded—we Remaned in the Town Two days then our Capt. march'd us up the Island to near King's Bridge—after our army had all

Cross'd the Enemy was Preparing for Further operations. Two Frigates came threw the Buttermilk Channel (15) and came to anchor off Turkel & Kips Bay to cover the landing of there army from Long Island—at this Time our Troops was Retreating up York Island—the Enemy advanceing till Harlem Hills—there our Troops Gave Battle (16)—the Battle was Severe for a Time. I was at the Morris House (17) when Major Hendey (18) was brought In mortally wounded who Soon Expir'd—we Repulsed the Enemy and kepd the Ground for a time—it was soon found that the Enemy was Preparing there Flotilla for the Sound—Gen. Swartout was orded to move off the Island and Take Post on Tippets neck on the East Side of Spitendevil (19)—at this Time I Got liberty to Visit West farms—when I Got there I saw the whole River from Hellgate to Flushing Bay Cover'd with Crafts Full of Troops, and my unkels Family moving off—at this Place Colonel Hand with his Rifle Reg't was station'd—as soon as I Got Back to the Company I was order'd with a small Escort to Procure Teams to move off our Stores and Baggage—the next day we arrived at the white Plains—the British Landed and was In new Rochelle—they moved on to near the Plains when Gen'l McDugal (20) engaged them at Chatterton Hill (21) and there He kepd the Ground—the Battle was Severe (22)—

the next day Capt. Van Vike of Fish Kill with a small Party Took the Road towards marroneck and fell in with a Party of English Horse and Exchang'd firing when our Capt. Rec'd a ball in the Head by the hat Band—they was too many for us, but we bore off our Capt. and Hid him in the Thicket and the next morning we went down and Bro't him off and Buried him—at this time the English army was Filing off to the left To the attack of Fort Washington (23) and our army moved to wright towards Peaks Kill the Chief of whom was order'd to Cross the River—by this Time fort Washington was Closely Invested—while the main Part of Enemy was Crossing the north River Washington thought Best to abandon Fort Lee, (24) as Fort Washington was Surrender'd (25)—at this Time the weather was Getting Very Cool. Gen'l Swartout Brigade was Posted on the South Side of the First mountain north of Peaks Kill. In December we had Very Cold weather and Severe Snow Storms—all this Time we was In Tents—we had to build Chimnies with Sods and Stone at one End of Tents—about the first Jan'y we was discharged. On my Discharge I was Presented with a Commistion In the Standing Army. I was A Good deal Surprized at it for I was Very little known and unsolisited for. I was so Strong a Patriot that I Very Readily accepted and was orderd To

Join Col'l Lewis Debois Regiment and Take his orders—I did and was Sent on the Recruting Service. I was kept on that Service for some time—I Took my First Station at Bedford, Westchester County and made my Home at Elijah Hunter's that winter and as uncle Leggett then was at Poundrige with his family I went there Part of the Time. In the Spring I Took my Station at and near Upper Salem. I made my Home at Isaac Nortons and in that and Spring of 1777 I Enlisted 45 Good men for army most of them for During the war—as I had been more successfull than many others I kept on that Duty—in May I obtain'd a Flag on my own a/c and Several others to Cross the Sound to Huntington, to fetch off some Familys and in the Company Two yong Ladys, a Miss Smith who was under Engagement to Joseph Titus and R. Morgan (26) who was also under Promise to myself. While we lay at Huntington Harbour the Famous Creditable Expedition of Governor Tryon (27) from New York landed at Compo between norwalk and Fairfield, march'd up Through the Country to Danbury where was a large Quantity of Provisons and Stores and Destroy'd the whole and the Town and on there way back they Burnt Richfield and Norwalk (28)—as soon as they Had accomplish'd that Enterprize they suffered us to depart—on our arrival at Norwalk we was astonish'd to

Behold the destruction and on arriving at Ridgfield we beheld Several of the wounded and Dying—one man had a ball threw his head and was Still alive—at Every breath the blood would blubber up Tho' he had been wounded before. I Remaned a few Days at Salem and 29th may was Married. In a few days I had to Join the Regiment at Fort montgomery (29) in the Highlands—there I Remaned till 4th Oct'r at night I was order'd with Gard and Boat down to Verplanks Point (30) to Recornoiter and observe the Conduct and movements of a British Frigate that had Got there. I Reman'd there all night with muffled oars—all was Quiet—at day I Return'd as orded and Reported—on 5th In the Evening Col'l Bruen was Sent down to the mountain first above Stoney Point—this was in Consequence of the Information of a large Force arrived there—they Tarried there Till morning—saw no movements and Return'd To Fort but as it seemed when our Gard left the mountain the Enemy ascended for the Col'l and his Gard had not Got there Breakfast before we had news the Enemy was ascending the mountain—a strong Party was orded To meet them—we met them in the hills and Bushes Two miles from the fort. Part had Got up the mountain and a part had Gone Round to attack the other part of Fort—we Faught them on a Retreat the Two miles till we Enter'd fort Clinton (31) on the west Side of Kill—the Two Forts where connected by a Bridge. Part of the force was orded over the bridge to montgomery—by this Time it was Very Dark. A Flag was sent and met by Col'l W. Livingston—there Demand was for a Surrender—the answer was they must Take it. Soon as the answer was Return'd Col. Cambell who Commanded the attack as soon as he was Informed the answer he Gave orders to spare none—they Came on Very Furiously and was Beat back and the Second and third Time when the Chief of line was Silenced all but the Redought I was in Commanded By Left. Col'l Bruen and Major Logan—at This Time we was Closely beset by Col'l Tunbull of Brittish and offered Good Quarters To Surrender and was accepted but the moment we Surrender'd they Crowded in upon us and began to Strip and Pillage what Ever we had on or about us. (32) I spoke To Tunbull myself Sir you Promist us Good Quarters—your Soldiers are stripping us and leaving us naked—his answer was They have Captur'd the Fort at the Risk of There lives and I Cant Restrane them—we had then to Submit—it was Fortunate For us that Cambell (33) who was for Putting all to the Sword Fell in the first Repulse—had he Survived I dought if any would have been Spared as We was Informed he was a Very Blood thirsty fellow. They lost In that

Enterprize Five Field officers and near 600 in all killed and a Grate many wounded—we lost But Trifling In killed and the most of Them after Surrender. We kill'd our number—we had not to Exceed from 6 to 700 and the half of them was new Recrutes and Raw millitia—that night on 6th Oct'r we was taking to the Barracks for Confinement—it So happend that I was put in the same Room that I occupide before the attack and my Baggage was safe But it was not long before Some of these Hungry officers Came in the Room and asking Silly Questions Took the liberty to Remove our Trunks out of the Room under the pretence of searching for arms—a Capt. J. Barns of Emmirick Core whose station was on the lines—when Barnes attempted to Remove the Trunk I claim'd and Told him I was the oldest son of John Leggett who was his Very Intimate Friend—he said he was only Going to search for arms—if he Found none would Return the Trunk but he did not find any I well know, but the next Day I Saw him Dress'd In my Clothes and what I most Regretted was a pair of Small Clothes of the Best make of Alsup & James Hunt Leather Breeches makers (34)—we was Captur'd on monday Evening 6th Octo'r—after Dark—we was kept in the Barrack Till wednesday in the Forenoon when we was taken from thence and Convaid Down the north River a little below Peaks

Kill and Put on Board of a Small Transport Ship Call'd the Mertell a Capt. Coats—we was in all about 300 officers and Privits Crowded up In Heaps between Decks being so Crowded that one Half Could not lie Down at the Same Time and So Close we Clould Scarsely Respire—a Grate Call was made For water—after Considerable Delay there was a Tub or Bucket put down but so foul that altho' we was almost Dying for Thirst Could not Drink it—at the same Time at low Tide the water along side was Drinkable—the officer who had the Gard at this Time on Deck was a Capt. or Lt. Robertson a son of Beverly Robertson whose Family then Lived at there Seat a little above Fort montgomery whose young Ladys and the mother the night Before the Fort was Taken Entertaind Gen'l Putnam (35) with that Pleasing attention that he forgot what he had been informed off the night before by myself. Had he attended and Sent over the Forces he had in his Power, we should not have been Taken. (36) Sir H. Clintons Effective Force at that onset was more than 3000 strong—while we was lying at anchor I formed a Plan of Going on shore. I had Prepared myself with a Rope by making it fast to the stantion and Crawling out feet foremost I Could lower myself in the water and swim for the East Shore I was fully confident I Could Gain the shore, But Col'l Brown and major Logan sit In to Perswade me from the attempt as it would Cause more severity with the Rest on board—There Treatment was so severe they had some Fear that we would attempt to Rize on the Gard For they Placed Two 4 Pounders at the Hatch and Loaded and Pointed down the Hatchway with a threat if we made the least noize they would Fire Down amongst us—we was kept so Close that Several was near sufficated—on Saturday morning the ship Came too at the Forrage Yard then kept at Bear market (37)—about 10 o'clock we was landed and the officers was seperated from the privits—they was sent To the Sugar House and the officers was Escorted to the main Gard then in the Old City Hall (38) at the Head of Broad st—all this Time we had nothing to Eat, but that night Col'l Wil'm Livingston sent a note to Mr. Simons (39) who kept a Public House at the Corner of nassaw st. By that means we was supply'd for that Time—on Sunday morning we was Escorted From that Prizen to the new Jail (40) Call'd The Provost Gard and at both Removes we was Very Highly Complemented on the way by the loyal subjects with all the hard names they Could think of, such as D——d Rebels and all other Fulsom names they Could think of. We did look Very Bad for the soldiers Stripp'd whatever we had on that was worth Taking off. I saved myself from being

Stripp'd for the morning we was orderd out to meet the Enemy I Put on the Poorest Clothes I had not wishing to dirty Good ones. On our way up nassaw st. near Maiden lane I espide my yongest sister Susan (41) standing on Mr. Norwood's (42) Stoop—as Soon as she Espide me She dropp'd *—I saw no more of Her—she Could not Get to see me but Sent me some Beding and Provisons that was of Grate Releaf—when we Got to Gard House we was Divided—12 of us was shut in the north Corner Room on the First floor and 13 was Put up on the second floor East Corner Room—after we was Shut in the Keeper Came In and Search'd and Took Everything we had about us not leaving a pen knife and on Wednesday they Threw in through the Hole in the Door Some Raw salt Beef and a little Damaged sea bread—as soon as the bread fell on the floor it Took legs and Ran in all Directions—so full of life—the flower was Very Filthy—more like Hog sty than anything else—This was Ten Days without Drawing Provisions after Taken—the Reason they Gave for their severe Treatment they said we had attempted to set the Barracks on Fire at our leaving them to go on board but the Case was soon Changed after the Capture of Burgoine and His army (43) of which we Got news In Prizen before the matter

* She *fainted*.

was known in the Citty Except by Some of Higher officers—the way the news was Convaid to the Prisen was in a Large Loaf of Bread—the statement on Paper and Placed in a loaf and Baked and was Sent Colonel William Livingston who was Taken with us—as soon as that was Read in the Congress Room, the whole Prizen Resounded with three Cheers (a)—the keeper was alarm'd with Such an uproar as he Call'd it—Hasten'd to the second floor to know what was the uproar—then He was Inform'd—he denide it and Said it was a D——d Rebbel lie—after this was fully known we was offer'd our Porlows as other officers on our Signing a Declaration wich they offer'd that we Did not attempt to leave fire as was against us—we then signed the Parole Bond and was Taken out of Prizen on the first day of Nov'r and Placed at different Houses in and about Bedford three miles from Brooklin—we was only in that Situation one Month for we was Too much In View of the Movements of British—from that we was Scatter'd to Various Parts—as for myself I was Put to Board at New Utrich where nine months and Lived Very well as the Family did—from thence was sent a ½ mile Further to make Room for some British officers. This was at the Time the British army was Retreating From Philadelphia. I was now at Rutgers Van brunt who was the High Sherif—while there I Had a severe attack of the Billious Fever. I was Confined Ten days—as soon as I was able to go about I was Removed from there to Mr. Abr'm Sniderkers at New Lots on the Jamaica Road about Eight miles from the ferry and was Very Comfortable situated—there I Remain'd till the 28th Day of Febuary when I obtain'd a Parole To Visit my family—the next day the first march Commenced a Very Severe Blustering snow storm and continued three weeks—all that Time I was detain'd—Could not Cross the Soun l—at last the weather became moderate and I Cross'd the Sound with Capt. Brewster to Fairfield, Connecticut, and when I arrived at Salem at Esq'r Leggett and there I Found my wife and Child well and Happy to meet again after 18 months absence and the Child Eleven months old who is now the wife of Capt. J. Breath (6) and the mother of nine Children. While I was a Prizener I Had Very Flattering offers if I would Join the British, or in otherwise would Take Protection and Go into Business in New York—my answer was, I have put my Hand to the Plow and Cant look Back—I shall Stand by my Country--We Remain'd at my unkels Esq'r Leggetts Till the Last april—I then Rented a small Tenement of Cap't Jabes Trusedal at north Salem, and Took an old Smithshop and went to work at my Trade. I Remain'd there Till the next Spring 1778. I then Rented a small farm of the commisioners of Sequestration and let it out on shares. In June my wife Rebecca was Confined with her second Daughter, Rebecca—the third Day She Expir'd—Then I was left alone with Two Small Children—the oldest but Twenty months. I soon Broke up House keeping and sold what few Goods I Had—my oldest Child Betsey I Took to my aunt Leggett and the Infant I Put to nurse to A Miss Hoxey who nursed with a bottle on Cows milk, and kept her three and a half years Till my second marriage. (16) In the year 1781 I was Exchanged when A General Exchange Took Place by a Resolution of Congress where there more of the Rank than was Requir'd—The Senior officer Had his Choice to Remain or Retire on Half Pay for life and to Receve all the Emollements as if still In the Ranks. In 1782 Major Jesse Brush was Commission'd By Govenor Clinton (17) To Go on to Long Iland In a Privite manner and Endevour to obtain Hard money on Loan For to supply some of the wants of the Troops who was Gratly Suffering for the want of Every thing and our Paper money was nothing. Maj'r Brush Took myself with him—we Remaind on the Island about three weeks In a Privit manner. In that Time He arranged with Several Persons for Specie and How to be Convey'd over the Sound. One day while there I spent the Day at Solomon Smiths; who

Resided on the Shore at the mouth of Smith Town Branch—the old man was a Grate Tory—he was a widower with Three Daughters—fine Girls and Good whigs. I Pass'd myself to the old man as a Butcher From N. York Looking for fat Cattle and Sheep—the old man Had been Plunder'd by Both sides he Told me and was Grately Distress'd and did not know what he Should do for Bread for the family. In The afternoon the old man rode out—the Girls was fearful in the afternoon that they might be Visited by Some of the Refugees from Fort Slongum (14)—Advised me to Retire up stairs Till night for Fear. In the Evning I Join'd our Party in the Bush whare we was supplide with a Good Repast by the Hands of the miss Smiths—and that afternoon arrangements was Enter'd with The Cap't of a Gard Vessel that lay in the Harbour To let us Pass with our Boat as we was only a Privit Party with no Hostile Intentions—he Gave us the Counter Sign and late in the Even'g we Road out of the harbour—by the Time we Got nearly ⅓ over the East wind Increasing Caused so much sea we found it necesary to Bare away for the long Island shore with our whale Boat, nine of us in her—we landed at a Place four miles East from whare we set out call'd the north Swamp—as soon as we landed the only one In the Company that knew whare to Go was myself. I Took T. Williams (15) with me to Procure some Provisons about one to the widow Floyds. I had been There before—we was supplide with what we wanted and Return'd to the Boat which Had been Carried up in the Edge of the Bushes and Turned Bottom up for it Came on to Rain and Storm—about 4 o'clock it held up—three of our Party went on the Hill under a Chesnut Tree. While there They was surprized by a Party of Refugee Torys they Then Rose over the hill Close upon the Rest of us. The day before we had Presented to us several of Rivington Royal Gazette—Lieut. Ketchum was overlooking one and I was Reading over his sholder when the stunning yell, Surrender you Dam Rebels and at the Instant fired a Voley down upon us—we all started for the Swamp not more than 5 or 6 Rods. I had not been more than seated in my mud and water Seat than the Cry was Here is the Track of one and another sung out the Same—from the Voice I knew it was mine—the first one Sung out here is one—who is it—maj'r Brush. Dont Hurt him was the Cry. I was Very Glad to hear That for as he was a Very active man I had my fears. By this Time the Persuer on my Track Came in full View of me—at the moment he brought his Gun from his Right Sholder on his left arm the Bayonet fixt my Thought was he then was a going To Seiver me. I determin'd in my mind to Surrender at the Instant he Gave another long Stride to another Bog which brought a bush between us—as he made His Step I was Rising up but I Soon Crouch'd again—So they Pass'd off—they then assembled a Round the boat—Some went after a waggon and Horses about a mile to the settlement and Return'd with it. Took the Boat and what Else there was and Drove off. (50) I Remain'd in my Soft seat for I dare not stir for fear some whare left to watch the Swamp—when it Got Quite Dark I Drew myself Softy out of the mud and sneak'd a Cross the Fealds to the House I had been at the night before and with the Soft Tap at the back part of the house window, it was not long before the window open'd—the Girls Saw my Situation—all wet and muddy. Miss Floyd Got her father's Cloths—he was a small man and I Considerable Stouter. I Had Difficulty to Get them on—when done I was Present'd with a flask of Cherry Bounce—the Cordal Came in Good time. Then follow'd other Refreshments—we then sat on the bed side—a yong Lady on Each Side—they then Gave me the account of the Refugees—they was in the Place some time, Press'd waggon and Horses, and with Boisterous behavour and Threats—from the Girls I first Learnt that Ketchum was Shot—after Talking some time I was furnishd with a Blanket and was waited upon by the Girls to Barn—

when we Came to the door Miss Floyd observed the Barn Door was not fast on the out Side as usal but Concluded some of the Party had been in after Straw—after Talking a while they bid me Good night and fastened the Door on the outside as usal—as soon as they was Gone and I Turn'd myself Round to Get in the Straw I was Surprized to hear footsteps in the Hay—the first Thought that occur'd the Refugees had Got in before me—the Door not fast on the outside strengthend that Idea—all that I Could do in that dillema was to Show Bold—therefore I hail'd Boldly, who is there—by the answer the Voice I new.* He Replide, "is that you Leggett"—my answer, yes—his Reply, God I am Glad—So there was Two Glad—he being in his wet Clothes I Gave my Blanket and Slepd in The Straw Very Comfortable Till morning—at an Early hour the Faithfull Girls Came with a Very Good Breefast, Coffe, Toost, and Beef Stake, of the best, and Plenty Good soft Peaches. They staid and Chatted Till Time to Prepare For Church about 4 miles at what is Call'd at head of the Branch—at there Return, we was Servd with Dinner—they was so Good as to Spend a Considerable of The afternoon—at Tea Time we was sarved in Stile—In the Coarse of the Day there was dispatched one of the sons To see if Capt. Bruster

* The name of this person was Timothy Williams.

was over—the answer was favorable. So in the Evening we was furnished with Two Horses and a Guide to Conduct us to the Place—we was Rec'd on board and by Day light In the morning we Landed at Black Rock, Fairfield, Glad that we was on Safe Ground—not long before, we heard from the Captives by some of there Friends that went to see them. They Express'd there Joye that I was not with them For on there march to Fort Slongum they met Doct. True whom I had caused to be stop'd the winter before near Bedford—he Drew his Sword and to show them How he would Serv'd me, he Cut and Hack'd the Bushes about him—they said he Had the appearance of Savage, and had I ben There He would have Put his Threats in Execution.

Abrm Leggett

NOTES.

(1) JOHN LEGGETT, the father of our author, was the son of William Leggett, of West Farms. His grandfather, Gabriel Leggett, the first of the name that settled in the State of New York, was born in England in 1635, and came to New York in the year 1661. He settled in that part of Westchester County, now known as West Farms, where he married Elizabeth, daughter of John Richardson, one of the first patentees of the place. She was still living in 1714. Gabriel Leggett's will is dated April 16, 1697. He left three sons—John, William and Gabriel—and one or more daughters. His son William had two sons—Abraham and John—the latter of whom was the father of our author, Major Leggett. The subject of this note was born in West Farms on the 4th day of Jan., 1732. His wife's maiden name was Sarah Alsop. She was the daughter of Thomas Alsop, of Newtown, L. I., who served for some years as a magistrate, and afterwards went into the mercantile business in New York, where

he died in Sept., 1743, in his 56th year. Her mother was Susannah, daughter of Robert Blackwell. Mr. Leggett was married to Miss Alsop on the 5th day of June, 1753. On the death of her husband in 1762, Mrs. Leggett returned to Newtown, her native place, where she subsequently married a Mr. Lawrence, and it is believed that she died in that town.

(2) These frigates were the MONTGOMERY, of 24 guns, *Capt. John Hodge*, and the CONGRESS, of 28 guns, *Capt. Thomas Grennall.* They were built at or near Poughkeepsie, on the Hudson river, in pursuance of a resolution of Congress of December 13, 1775. They never got to sea, as the British held the mouth of the river from August, 1776, to November, 1783. In the year 1777, when Sir Henry Clinton took the forts in the highlands, these two vessels, having been ordered down for the defence of the chain, were burnt by their crews to prevent them from falling into the hands of the enemy.

(3) COL. BERNARDUS SWARTWOUT was the son of Bernardus Swartwout, a prominent merchant of New York, and was born on the 26th day of September, 1761. After the Revolution, he went with his father into the brick and lumber business in New York city, in which he continued for many years. He was one of the original members of the New York State Society of the Cincinnati, and in the year 1794 was elected its Assistant Treasurer. In the year following, he held the office of Secretary of the same organization. He died at Greenburgh, Westchester County, N. Y., on Friday, October 8th, 1824, in the 69th year of his age. His remains were interred in the graveyard of the Dutch Reformed Church at Sleepy Hollow.

(4) "The British troops landed on Staten Island on the 3d July, 1776. A part of the stock had been taken off. The inhabitants, who were about 350 men, were supposed to be generally opposed to the Revolution."

Heath's Memoirs, p. 48.

(5) "The British commanders, having resolved to make their first attempt on Long Island, landed their troops, estimated at about 24,000 men, at Gravesend Bay, to the right of the Narrows, on the 22d Aug., 1776. The Americans, to the amount of 15,000, under Maj. Gen. Sullivan, were posted on a peninsula between Mill Creek, a little above Red Hook, and an elbow of the East River, called Wallabout Bay. Here they had erected strong fortifications, which were separated from New York by the East River, at a distance of a mile. A line of intrenchments from the Mill Creek enclosed a large space of ground, on which stood the American camp, near the village of Brooklyn. This line was separated by a range of hills, covered with thick woods, which intersect the country from west to east, terminating on the east, near Jamaica."

Holmes' Annals, Vol. 2, p. 245.

(6) WILLIAM ALEXANDER (commonly known as LORD STERLING), was born in the city of New York in the year 1726, and was the son of James Alexander, a Scotchman, who took refuge in America in 1716, after an active espousal, during the previous year, of the cause of the Pretender. His mother was the widow of David Provoost, better known in the city of New York a little more than a century ago, as "Ready Money Provoost." The subject of our sketch received an excellent mathematical education, and obtained some distinction as a man of science. In the French and Indian war

he acted as Aid-de-camp and Secretary to Gen. Shirley, and at the close of the war accompanied him to England. He returned to America in 1761, and soon after married the daughter of Philip Livingston. In March, 1776, he was appointed by Congress a Brigadier-General, and in April following took command at New York. He was taken prisoner at the battle of Brooklyn, but was soon after exchanged, and in February following, was appointed Major-General. He was subsequently in the battles of Brandywine, Germantown and Monmouth, and in 1781 was stationed at Albany, to command the Northern army. In the year following he made Philadelphia his head-quarters, and in the Spring he again took command of the northern troops, and located himself at Albany. He died there on the 15th January, 1783, from an attack of the gout, in the 57th year of his age.

(:) MAJ. GEN. JOHN SULLIVAN was born in Berwick, in the State of Maine, on the 17th day ot Feb., 1740. After studying law he established himself in the profession in New Hampshire. Turning his attention to military affairs, he received, in 1772, the commission of Major, and in 1775, that of Brigadier-General. The next year he was sent to Canada, and on the death of Gen. Thomas, succeeded him in command of the army there. In this year he was promoted to the rank of Major-General, and was soon after captured by the British in the battle on Long Island. He was subsequently exchanged, and rejoined the army. At the battles of Trenton, Brandywine and Germantown, he commanded a division, and was the sole commander of an expedition to Newport, R. I., which failed through want of coöperation of the French fleet. In 1779 he commanded an expedition against the Indians. He was afterwards a member of Congress, and was for three years President of New Hampshire. In 1789 he was appointed a judge of the District Court, and continued in that office until his death, which occurred Jan. 23d, 1795.

(8) THE FLATBUSH HILLS—the chain of hills or high ground running across the Island, in a northeasterly direction from New Utrecht on the south, towards Hempstead Bay on the north, forming the boundary line between Brooklyn and New Utrecht—a natural line of defense.

(9) The MILLPOND here mentioned is that of Brower's Mill, the oldest of the eight tide-mills which until within a few years existed in the boundaries of Brooklyn. The pond was formed by damming off the head of Gowanus Kil, or Creek. This mill, in 1661, was held conjointly by Isaac de Forest and Adam Brower, the latter of whom subsequently became its sole owner. It was probably held on a lease, as the land belonged to Jan Evertsen Bout, who in 1667 gave "the corn and meadows, and place whereon the mill is grounded," to the children of Brower. The mill subsequently came into the hands of Freeke, from whence it is often called "Freeke's Mill," also as the "Old Gowanus Mill." There is a good representation of it in "Lossing's Field Book of the Revolution," vol. 2, p. 810.

(10) The battle of Brooklyn took place on the 28th day of August, 1776, and resulted in the complete victory of the British. The total loss of the Americans was estimated at more than 3,000 men in killed, wounded and prisoners. Among the latter were Major-General Sullivan, and Brigadier-

Generals Lord Sterling and Woodhull. Almost the entire regiment of Maryland, consisting of young men of the best families in that province, was cut to pieces. Six pieces of cannon fell into the power of the victors. The loss of the English was very inconsiderable; in killed, wounded and prisoners, it did not amount to 400 men.

For accounts of the battle, see—

Freeman's Journal, Sept. 28, 1776.
Thompson's Hist. Long Island, vol. i., p. 216.
Onderdonk's Suffolk and Kings Counties, p. 132.
Gordon, vol. ii., p. 306.
Holmes' Am. Annals, vol. ii., p. 245.
Samuel Ward's paper. Knickerbocker Mag., vol. xiii., p. 281.
Martin's Narrative, p. 17.

(11) FORT PUTNAM, now known as Fort Green, and Washington Square, was a redoubt with five guns, and commanded the East River and the roads approaching Brooklyn from the interior. An intrenchment extended from Fort Putnam northwesterly, down the hill to a spring (in 1852 in a tanning yard, with a pump in it, near the intersection of Portland street and Flushing Avenue). This spring was then on the verge of the Wallabout.

Lossing's Field Book of the Revolution, vol. ii., p. 806.

(12) The OLD STONE CHURCH here referred to, was the Dutch Reformed Church, erected about the year 1706, in the middle of the road from the Ferry to Flatbush (now Fulton-street, near the vicinity of the burying-ground, between Hoyt and Smith streets), and was the second church edifice which had stood on that spot. The old church was square in form, and was built of stone. It had high windows, with painted

glass of a grape-vine pattern. It had a sort of hump-backed roof, surmounted by a cupola. It was the "alarm post" of the American forces during the battle of Brooklyn, and until after the Revolution, the only church edifice in the town.

(13) This difficult movement was effected with great skill and judgment, and with complete success. Heaven remarkably favored the fugitive army. A southwest wind springing up at eleven, essentially facilitated its passage from the island to the city; and a thick fog, hanging over Long Island from about two in the morning, concealed its movements from the enemy, who were so near that the sound of their pickaxes and shovels was heard. In about half an hour after, the fog cleared away, and the enemy were seen taking possession of the American lines. Gen. Washington, as far as possible, inspected everything. From the commencement of the action on the morning of the 27th, until the troops were safely across East River, he never closed his eyes, and was almost constantly in the saddle. His wisdom and vigilance, with the interposing favor of Divine Providence, saved the army from destruction.

Holmes' Annals, vol. ii., p. 248.
Gordon, vol. ii., p. 314.

(14) THOMAS MIFFLIN was born in Philadelphia about the year 1744, of parents who were Quakers. He engaged early in opposition to the measures of the British Parliament. In 1772 he was a representative of Philadelphia in the Colonial Assembly. In 1774 he was a member of the First Congress, and in August, 1775, was appointed Quartermaster-General. He was with Gen. Washington at Cambridge, and in the Spring of 1776 was commissioned a Brigadier-General in the

Continental army. He was made Major-General in Feb., 1777, and he continued in service during the war. In 1783 he was a representative in Congress, and in the autumn of that year was appointed its president. In 1787 he was a member of the Convention which formed the Constitution of the United States, and his name is affixed to that instrument. In October, 1788, he succeeded Dr. Franklin as President of the Supreme Executive Council of Pennsylvania, in which station he continued till October, 1790. He was elected the first governor of Pennsylvania, under the provisions of the new Constitution, and held the office for nine years consecutively. By his personal exertions he greatly assisted in quelling the "Whisky Insurrection," in 1794. Gen. Mifflin died at Lancaster, Pa., Jan. 20, 1800, at the age of 56.

(15) BUTTERMILK CHANNEL—the name given to the stream of water between the Red Hook Point and Governor's Island. There is a strong tradition that in early times this stream was fordable, but that this was not the case is clearly disproved by reference to B. Ratzer's Map of New York City, made in 1766, [see *Valentine's Manual*, 1854, at p. 320,] on which a depth was given at that time to the channel of three fathoms of water.

(16) The action at Harlem Plains took place on the 16th September, 1776, and was a very spirited affair, reflecting the highest credit on the part of the Americans. The following account of the action is given by one who was an eye witness and participator in the contest:

"The next day, in the forenoon, the enemy, as we expected, followed us 'hard up,' and were advancing through a level field; our rangers and some few other light troops, under the command of Colonel Knowlton, of Connecticut, and Major Leitch, of (I believe) Virginia, were in waiting for them. Seeing them advancing, the rangers, &c., concealed themselves in a deep gully overgrown with bushes; upon the western verge of this defile was a post and rail fence, and over that the forementioned field. Our people let the enemy advance until they arrived at the fence, when they arose and poured in a volley upon them. How many of the enemy were killed and wounded could not be known, as the British were always as careful as Indians to conceal their losses. There were, doubtless, some killed, as I myself counted nineteen ball-holes through a single rail of the fence at which the enemy were standing when the action began. The British gave back and our people advanced into the field. The action soon became warm. Colonel Knowlton, a brave man, and commander of the detachment, fell in the early part of the engagement. It was said by those who saw it, that he lost his valuable life by unadvisedly exposing himself singly to the enemy. In my boyhood I had been acquainted with him; he was a brave man and an excellent citizen. Major Leitch fell soon after, and the troops, who were then engaged, were left with no higher commanders than their Captains, but they still kept the enemy retreating.

Our regiment was now ordered into the field, and we arrived on the ground just as the retreating enemy were entering a thick wood, a circumstance as disagreeable to them as it was agreeable to us at that period of the war. We soon came to action with them. The troops engaged, being reinforced by our regiment, kept them still retreating, until they found shelter under the cannon of some of their shipping.

lying in the North river. We remained on the battle-ground till nearly sunset, expecting the enemy to attack us again, but they showed no such inclination that day. The men were very much fatigued and faint, having had nothing to eat for forty-eight hours,—at least the greater part were in this condition, and I among the rest. While standing on the field, after the action had ceased, one of the men near the Lieut. Colonel complained of being hungry; the Colonel, putting his hand into his coat pocket, took out a piece of an ear of Indian corn, burnt as black as a coal, 'Here,' said he to the man complaining, 'eat this and learn to be a soldier.'"

Martin's Narrative, p. 32.

See accounts of this engagement also in

Lossing's Field Book, vol. ii., p. 818.
Graydon's Memoirs, p. 199.
Holmes' Annals, vol. ii., p. 249.

(12) The "MORRIS HOUSE," which is still standing, is located on the bank of the Harlem river, at what is now 169th-street, a little below the High Bridge of the Croton Aqueduct. It was an elegant mansion, and was, at the commencement of the Revolution, the residence of Col. Roger Morris. He, siding with the King, fled to the residence of Beverly Robinson in the highlands, and his house became the headquarters of Washington. The house and lands adjoining, after the war, became the property of Madame Eliza B. Jumel, subsequently the widow of Aaron Burr. Here she lived many years, and here she died, Sunday morning, July 16, 1865, in her 92d year.

(13) MAJOR THOMAS HENLY was a native of Charlestown, Mass. He was the Aid-de-camp to Gen. Heath. He volun-

teered to join the party under Lieut.-Col. Jackson, who, on the 22d September, 1776, with 240 men, in three flat-boats, made a descent on Montresor's, now Randall's Island, of which the British had taken possession. The troops in one boat only, effected a landing, and these were driven back with the loss of fourteen men killed, wounded and missing. Henly behaved with great courage, but was shot just as he was entering the boat, and instantly expired. He was buried below a hill where a redoubt had been thrown up in the road. Here Col. Knowlton, who had been killed at the engagement at Harlem Plains, was buried, and Major Henly was laid by his side.

(19) SPYT DEN DYVEL CREEK, with the Harlem river, of which it is a part, forms Manhattan Island, on which the city of New York is built. It is about thirteen miles above New York, and flows into the Hudson. It is here that Irving laid the death of Antony Van Corlaer, the trumpeter of the chivalrous Governor Stuyvesant. It is therefore a classic spot to the lovers of mirth.

(20) MAJOR-GENERAL ALEXANDER M'DOUGALL was the son of a Scotchman who sold milk in the city of New York, and the son, when a boy, assisted the father in the business. The subject of our sketch took an early stand on the side of the colonists, and when the war broke out he joined the army. In August, 1776, he was appointed a Brigadier-General, and in the month of October of the year following, he was commissioned as Major-General. He commanded the Americans in the action at White Plains in 1776, and was in the battle at Germantown in the autumn of 1777. In 1781 he wa

elected a delegate to Congress, and subsequently was chosen a member of the New York State Senate. He died in the month of June, 1786.

(21) CHATTERTON HILL lies on the northeast corner of the town of Greenburgh, in Westchester County. The Chatterton family, from whom the hill derives its name, have been long residents of Greenburgh. A member of this family was settled on the hill as early as 1731. It was upon this hill that the chief part of the battle of White Plains was fought.

(22) The battle of White Plains was fought on the 28th October, 1776. The Americans were commanded by Gen. McDougall, and the British by Gen. Leslie. The action was but partial, and was undecided. The loss on both sides was about equal. Among the persons wounded on the side of the British, was Lieutenant-Col. Musgrave, commanding the light infantry; among the killed was Lieutenant-Col. Cars, of the 35th, and Capt. Evelyn, of the 4th regiment. Among the wounded on the side of the Americans, was Col. Smallwood. "While the engagement was going on," says Ramsay, "the baggage of the Americans was moved off in full view of the British army. Soon after this, Washington changed his front; his left wing stood fast, and his right fell back to some hills. In this position, which was an admirable one in a military point of view, he both desired and expected an action; but Gen. Howe declined it, and drew off his forces towards Dobb's Ferry. The Americans afterwards retired to North Castle."

Ramsay's Am. Rev., vol. i., p. 314.

The following account is given by one who participated in the engagement:

"When we arrived at the camp, the troops were all parading. Upon inquiry, we found that the British were advancing upon us. We flung our turnip plunder into the tent—packed up our things, which was easily done, for we had but a trifle to pack, and fell into the ranks. Before we were ready to march, the battle had begun. Our regiment then marched off, crossed a considerable stream of water which crosses the plain, and formed behind a stone wall in company with several other regiments, and waited the approach of the enemy. They were not far distant: at least, that part of them with which we were quickly after engaged. They were constructing a sort of bridge to convey their artillery, &c., across the before mentioned stream. They however soon made their appearance in our neighbourhood. There was in our front, about ten rods distant, an orchard of apple trees. The ground on which the orchard stood was lower than the ground that we occupied, but was level from our post to the verge of the orchard, when it fell off so abruptly that we could not see the lower parts of the trees. A party of Hessian troops, and some English, soon took possession of this ground; they would advance so far as just to show themselves above the rising ground, fire, and fall back, and reload their muskets. Our chance upon them was, as soon as they showed themselves above the level ground, or when they fired, to aim at the flashes of their guns—their position was as advantageous to them as a breast work. We were engaged in this manner for some time, when finding ourselves flanked and in danger of being surrounded, we were compelled to make a hasty retreat from the stone wall. We lost comparatively speaking, very few at the fence; but when forced to retreat, we lost, in killed and wounded, a considerable number. One man who belonged to our company, when we marched from the parade, said, 'Now, I am going out to the field to be killed;' and he said more than once afterwards, that he should be killed; and he was—he was shot dead on the field. I never saw a man so prepossessed with the idea of any mishap as he was. We fell back a little distance and made a stand; detached parties engaging in almost every direction. We did not come in contact with the enemy again that day, and just at night we fell back to our encampment. In the course of the afternoon the British took possession of a hill on the right of our encampment, which had in the early part of the day been occupied by some of the New York troops. This hill overlooked the one upon which we were, and was not more than half or three-fourths of a mile distant. The enemy had several pieces of field artillery upon this hill, and, as might be expected, entertained us with their music all the evening. We entrenched ourselves where we now lay, expecting another attack. But the British were very civil, and indeed they generally were, after they had received a check from Brother Jonathan, for any of their rude actions; they seldom repeated them, at least, not till the affair that caused the reprimand, had ceased in some measure to be remembered."

Martin's Narrative, p. 40-41.

See also accounts of the battle in

Gordon's Am. War, vol. ii., p. 339-343.
Holmes' Am. Annals, vol. ii., p. 250.
Pennsylvania Evening Post, Nov. 14, 1776.

(23) FORT WASHINGTON was situated on the east side of the Hudson, about ten miles from the city of New York, and its

remains are still to be seen. The fort consisted of a strong earth-work, covering with its revelins, several acres, and mounting twenty heavy guns, besides sundry smaller pieces, and mortars. On the promontory beneath it (Jeffrey's Hook), where the telegraph mast now stands, was a redoubt, intended to act as a covering defence to chevaux-de-frise, which there crossed the channel to Fort Lee, on the opposite side of the river. A short distance northward of Fort Washington, between 195th and 198th-streets, is the site of a small redoubt of two guns, taken by the British on the morning of the capture of Fort Washington, and afterwards strengthened by them, and named Fort Tryon. Still further north, about two miles above Fort Washington, at 217th-street, stood another two-gun redoubt, called Cock Hill Fort, which was taken by the British at the same time.

(24) FORT LEE was situated on the west side of the Hudson, about ten miles above the city of New York, and nearly opposite Fort Washington. The site of the old fort was upon the bluff above, where commences the Pallisade range. The fort was hastily evacuated by its garrison after the fall of Fort Washington, and most of its artillery, a considerable part of the tents and baggage, and some hundred barrels of flour, were taken, besides six officers and staff, and some ninety-nine privates.

(25) When the American army retreated to White Plains, it was decided to leave a large garrison in Fort Washington, in order to prevent the enemy from ascending the Hudson River. This fort was on a high piece of ground, very difficult of ascent, especially towards the north. The fortifications,

though not sufficient to resist heavy artillery, were believed to be in a condition which would prevent any attempt to carry them by storm. The garrison consisted of some of the best troops in the American army, and the commander, Col. Magaw, was a brave and intelligent officer, in whose courage and skill great confidence was placed. The attack on the fort was made on the 16th November, 1776. Four divisions of the enemy, led by their principal officers, attacked it in four different quarters. The garrison, and particularly the riflemen, under Col. Rawlings, behaved bravely. The Hessians were several times driven back with great loss; but these combined and vigorous attacks were at length successful. The ammunition in the fort being nearly exhausted, and all the outposts driven in, the commander, on being a second time summoned, agreed to capitulate on honorable terms. After the surrender, the garrison, numbering about 2,000 men, were crammed the first night for safe-keeping into a barn on the Morris farm, then the British Head-quarters. The night was warm and the feted air engendered from so many breathing lungs, became positively insupportable. There was a constant cry for water, which was not withheld; but the pressure prevented many from reaching it, and they had to endure the most agonizing thirst the whole night. Capt. Graydon, of the Pennsylvania line, who was one of the prisoners, informs us in his memoirs, "that he could liken the scene to none other than the 'Black Hole of Calcutta.'" To add to their distress, they had to endure the jeers and taunts of their enemies, without the power of resentment. The next day the prisoners were marched to the city of New York, where they were thrown into prisons and prison-ships, and in those miserable, loathsome dungeons, a large portion of them died from hunger and disease. Gen. Washington was situated where he could view several parts of the attack, and he exclaimed at the barbarities practiced by the British. It is said that when he beheld his men bayoneted, and in that way killed, while begging for quarter, he could not refrain from tears. The loss of Fort Washington was the severest blow the Americans had then felt, and spread a deep gloom for a while over the American cause.

Graydon's Memoirs, p. 197-210.
Ramsay's Am. Rev., vol. i., p. 395.
Gordon's Am. War, vol. ii., p. 349.
Holmes' Am. Annals, vol. ii., p. 250.
New Hampshire Gazette, Dec. 10, 1776.

(26) REBECCA MORGAN was the daughter of John Morgan, of Huntington, L. I., who was by occupation a farmer. She was born in Huntington on the 7th day of June, 1758. She was married to Major Leggett, at North Salem, Westchester County, N. Y., on the 29th May, 1777. She died June 12th, 1780. She left two daughters, viz.:

1. BETSEY, born April 1, 1778; married to Capt. James Breath, October 16, 1800; died, Feb. 12, 1859.
2. REBECCA, still living, born June 10, 1780; married Ovid Goldsmith, May 12, 1827. Mr. Goldsmith was captain of a vessel, and went whaling. He subsequently left the sea, and became an inspector of lime in Athens, Greene County, N. Y. He died of cholera, on the 18th August, 1832. They had no children.

(27) LIEUTENANT-GENERAL WILLIAM TRYON was bred to the profession of arms. He became Lieutenant and Captain of the 1st Regiment of Foot Guards, October 15 1751, and on

the 30th September, 1758, was raised to a Captaincy, and to be a Lieutenant-Colonel in the Guards. In 1764 he was appointed Lieutenant-Governor of North Carolina, where he arrived October 27th, and on the death of Governor Dobbs in 1765, he succeeded him in command of that colony. He continued to administer the government there until July, 1771, when he was made Governor of New York. He was promoted to a Coloneley in the army, May 25, 1772; became 3d Major of the Guards, June 8, 1775; Major-General, August 29, 1777; and Colonel of the 7th Regiment, May 25, 1778. His career in America was as notorious as it was odious. On the 21st March, 1780, he resigned the government of New York, and was succeeded by Gen. Robertson. Gen. Tyron returned to England, and on the 20th November, 1782, was appointed Lieutenant-General, and on the 16th August, 1783, Colonel of the 29th Foot. He died at his house, in Upper Grosvenor-street, London, on the 27th January, 1788, and his remains were deposited in the family vault at Twickenham, England.

(22) The burning of Danbury, Connecticut, took place on the 26th April, 1777. The British force amounted to about 2,000 men, and was under the command of Major-General Tryon. "He embarked at New York, and passing through Long Island Sound, landed at Compo, between Fairfield and Norwalk, whence he advanced through the country, almost undisturbed, to Danbury. On his approach, Col. Huntington, who had occupied the town with 100 militia and continental troops, retired to a neighboring height, where he waited for reenforcements. The British destroyed 18 houses, 800 barrels of pork and beef, 800 barrels of flour, 2,000 bushels of grain,

and 1,700 tents. Generals Wooster, Arnold and Silliman, hastily collecting several hundred of the inhabitants, proceeded that night through a heavy rain to Bethel, about eight miles from Danbury. The next morning they divided their troops, and General Wooster, with about 300 men, fell in their rear, while Arnold, with about 500, by a rapid movement, took post in their front at Ridgefield. Wooster coming up with them about eleven in the morning of the 27th, attacked them with great gallantry. A sharp skirmish ensued, in which he was mortally wounded, and his troops were compelled to give way. The enemy proceeded to Ridgefield, where Arnold, who had barricaded the road, warmly disputed the passage; but after a skirmish of nearly an hour, being compelled to give way, he retreated to Saugatuck, about three miles east of Norwalk. The royalists, having remained that night at Ridgefield, set fire to the place, and early next morning resumed their march. Arnold met them again about eleven, and a continued skirmishing was kept up until five in the afternoon, when, on their making a stand at a hill near their ships, the Americans charged them with intrepidity, but were repulsed and broken. The enemy immediately re-embarked for New York. Their killed, wounded and missing amounted to about 170; the loss of the Americans was not admitted to exceed 100." This predatory excursion was shortly after retaliated by Lieutenant-Colonel Return J. Meigs, in the surprise of Sag Harbour, and the destruction of a large amount of property at that place.

Holmes' American Annals, vol. ii., p. 263.

Another writer, in alluding to the destruction of property, etc., by the British at Danbury, says:

"We had an ample opportunity to see the devastation

caused there by the British. The town had been laid in ashes, a number of the inhabitants murdered and cast into their burning houses, because they presumed to defend their persons and property, or to be avenged on a cruel, vindictive, invading enemy. I saw the inhabitants, after the fire was out, endeavouring to find the burnt bones of their relatives amongst the rubbish of their demolished houses. The streets, in many places, were literally flooded by the fat which ran from the piles of barrels of pork burnt by the enemy."

Martin's Narrative, p. 46.

See also

Connecticut Journal, April 30, 1777.
Pennsylvania Journal, May 14, 1777.
Gaine, May 12 and 19, 1777
Pennsylvania Gazette, May 14, 1777.
Pennsylvania Eve. Post, May 22, 1777.

([illegible]) FORT MONTGOMERY was on the west side of the Hudson River, opposite St. Anthony's Nose. The fort was constructed pursuant to a resolution of Congress of August 18, 1775, and was intended for defence of the river. Huge booms and a powerful iron chain were constructed, and stretched across the river from this point. This chain was about 1,800 feet long, and was composed of links a little over two feet in length, weighing each 140 pounds, and was fixed to huge blocks on each shore and under the cover of batteries on both sides of the river. It was manufactured by Peter Townsend, of Chester, and several links of it are still preserved, and are to be seen at the Head-quarters at Newburgh. The fortifications and obstructions were all made under the direction of Capt. Thomas Machin, a gallant officer of the Revolution, and an engineer of rare skill and genius.

(30) VERPLANCK'S POINT derives its name from Philip Verplanck, who married the only granddaughter and heiress of Stephen Van Cortlandt, who purchased the land from the Indians. Previous to this it had borne the name of Meahagh. The point rises gradually from the river's brink, and terminates in a bold bluff of forty or fifty feet in height. This was the spot where Hendrick Hudson first brought his ship, the Half Moon, to anchor, after leaving the mouth of the Hudson River. A small fortification once existed on the western extremity of the point, and was called Fort Lafayette. Verplanck's Point was at one time the head-quarters of Gen. Washington.

(31) FORT CLINTON stood on the west side of the Hudson, and nearly adjoining Fort Montgomery, the two forts being separated by a creek, over which a bridge had been erected. Fort Clinton was erected pursuant to a resolution of Congress of August 18, 1775, and was intended to defend the river against the approach of any hostile naval force. It stood upon an eminence, and was the principal fort in the Highlands.

(32) Forts Montgomery and Clinton were considered the main defences of the highlands, and were placed under the command of Governor Clinton, and garrisoned with the best troops. Collateral efforts were made to render the river impassable to the enemy's ships. Chevaux-de-frize were sunk, a boom was extended from shore to shore, and armed vessels were stationed in positions where they could act with the most powerful effect. These precautions, added to the natural strength of the forts, determined Sir Henry Clinton, who considered their subjugation indispensable to the success of his

further designs, to employ stratagem, in preference to an open and unequivocal demonstration to possess himself of holds which required little more than vigilance to render them unconquerable. By a succession of deceptive movements, therefore, he impressed General Putnam, who commanded that district, with a belief that his object was Fort Independence, which was situated four or five miles below Fort Montgomery, and on the opposite side of the river. Having drawn the attention of Gen. Putnam to Fort Independence, Sir Henry Clinton debarked the troops intended for the attack on the west side of Stony Point, and marching them into the rear of Fort Montgomery, commenced the assault. Alarmed by the noise of the firing, Gen. Putnam discovered his error, and detached a reinforcement of five hundred men to the garrisons which were in such imminent peril; but, before their arrival, Fort Montgomery was in the possession of the British troops. Governor Clinton adopted every means which skill could devise, or valor execute, to save the posts intrusted to his charge; and, in consequence of the extensiveness of his lines, he was compelled to leave them but imperfectly manned at many points. He defended them with effect, until darkness came on, when the enemy succeeded in making an entrance. The loss of the garrison was stated at 250 men, and that of the British was said to be greater. After the fall of Forts Montgomery and Clinton, Gen. Putnam retired to Fishkill, and waited for such reinforcements as might enable him to resume offensive operations, while the British general (Vaughan) proceeded up the river, and destroyed Continental Village and Esopus. On the surrender of Gen. Burgoyne, however, he made a retrograde movement, and, after reducing Forts Montgomery and Clinton to ashes, returned to New York.

The following articles in regard to this subject, we find published in the papers of the day:

"I have now the pleasure to felicitate you on our taking the forts Montgomery and Clinton by storm. It was effected last night [Oct. 6]. The garrisons in both places consisted of twelve hundred rebels. Of our detachment, we lost Mungo Campbell, Lieutenant Colonel of the 52d, and Major Sill of the 63d. Major Grant, of the New York Volunteers, was killed a little before the attack, which was commanded by Colonel Mungo Campbell. My old acquaintance, George Turnbull, late captain in the Royal American Regiment, was ordered to take the command of Grant's corps. He has acquired great honor, being the first that entered Fort Montgomery, after losing one officer and eight privates. Sir Henry Clinton, who himself narrowly escaped the enemy's grape-shot, in consideration of his very gallant behavior, has appointed him Lieutenant-Colonel Commandant of the New York Volunteers, in room of the brave Major Grant. The gallant Count Gabrouski, lately arrived from England, has died of his wounds. Amongst the prisoners is Colonel William Allison, of the Drowned Lands, whose son was killed in the fort. This person is a member of the provincial congress for the State (as it is termed) of New York. Also young William Livingston, late of New York, in the profession of the law. A great part of the twelve hundred rebels, who garrisoned the forts Montgomery and Clinton, or were not killed or prisoners, made their escape, as it was very dark when the forts were taken. The forbearance and humanity shown by all the troops to the rebels after they became their conquerors, was astonishing; and savored of that benign temper which ever characterizes the army of Great Britain."

Gaine, Oct. 11, 1777.

"NEW YORK. *November 3.*

Saturday, sen' night the Bridge laid over the Clove, between the Forts Montgomery and Clinton, was destroyed; and the Troops, after demolishing the latter, embarked on board the Transports, and arrived here the next evening."

Gaine, Monday, November 3, 1777.

see also

New York Journal, May 11, 1778.
Ruttenber's Obstructions on the Hudson River, p. 64.
Gordon's American War, vol. ii., p. 555.
Holmes' American Annals, vol. ii., p. 276.
Simms' Hist. Schoharie Co., p. 550.
Eager's Orange Co., pp. 571–579 and 594–6.
Sparks' Washington, vol. v., pp. 471–476.

(33) The following advertisement we take from one of the newspapers of the period:

"PUBLIC AUCTION.—

At the Coffee House on Wednesday, will be sold the personal effects of the late Col. Campbell.

On Thursday, at 11 o'Clock at the regimental store in Queen-street, near Beekman-slip, the regimental effects of the late Lieut. Col. Campbell.

All persons who have any regimental demands on the effects of the late Lieut. Col. Campbell, of the 52d regt. are desired forthwith to deliver an account of the same to the quarter master of said regt. that they may be satisfied."

Gaine, Monday, November 17, 1777.

(34) ALSOP HUNT and JAMES HUNT were leather dressers and glove and breeches manufacturers in the city of New York. They carried on the business under the firm-name of

Alsop & James Hunt. In 1789 and 1790 they were located at No. 212 Queen, now Pearl-street, and in 1791 were at No. 54 Water-street. They seem to have dissolved in the course of this year, as we find Alsop in the year following carrying on the business alone, at No. 212 Queen-street. James and his wife died of the yellow fever about the year 1798. Alsop moved to New Jersey, where he died some years later.

(55) MAJOR-GENERAL ISRAEL PUTNAM was the son of Capt. Joseph Putnam, and was born in Salem, Mass., on the 7th day of January, 1718. His boyhood was passed in the labors of a farm and in athletic exercises, in the latter of which he seems to have excelled. His biographer, Mr. Cutter, informs us that he was also remarkably successful in climbing trees, robbing nests, and causing sorrow to small birds. In 1739, being then in his 21st year, Putnam moved to Pomfret, Conn., where he subsequently pursued the avocation of a farmer. It is here that he is said to have been engaged in the conflict with a famous she-wolf, and it is to this day an unsettled point which acquired from the contest the greatest celebrity, Putnam or the wolf. His next service was in the old French war, in which he commanded a company of Provincials, and where he did some duty as a scout; but he seems to have been mostly distinguished at this period for his remarkable escapes from death, first by the bullet, then by the tomahawk, and lastly at the stake. By the kindly interposition of Col. Schuyler, who represented him to be "*a useless old man,*" Putnam was at length released from imprisonment, and at the conclusion of the war, returned to his farm. Soon after the battle of Lexington, Putnam obtained command of a regiment of Connecticut troops, and in a short time after, by some cute manage-

ment or unaccountable good fortune, was promoted to the rank of a Major-General. We next hear of him at the battle of Bunker's Hill, not as one of the gallant combatants, but as a spectator of that eventful conflict, and the only service he appears to have rendered on that occasion, was in keeping watch over a lot of spades, pick-axes, and other intrenching tools. At the battle of Brooklyn in 1776, he appears as Commander-in-Chief of the American forces, and here, by his neglect to guard the main passes, he allowed the enemy to gain his rear, and the result was the complete defeat of the Continental army, the loss of some 3,000 men killed, wounded and captured, and the subsequent occupation of New York by the enemy. After this, Putnam was placed in command at the Highlands, and here, instead of profiting by his experience at Long Island, he repeated the mistake he made there, and by his neglect, lost those important posts, Forts Montgomery and Clinton, with some 2,000 of the best troops in the army. In consequence of Putnam's incapacity, which now became too evident to be longer concealed, he was at length relieved of command, and ordered to Connecticut on recruiting service, a position much better suited to his abilities. Putnam's last command was at West Point, where he did not long continue, for he was soon after seized with a paralytic affection, which disqualified him for further duty. He took up his residence at Brooklyn, Conn., where he died on the 29th day of May, 1790, when about 72 years of age. Gen. Putnam was a man of strong frame and robust constitution. He was quick in his temper, rough in his manner, and though lamentably ignorant, very conceited and headstrong. Though fitted very well for a farmer, a hunter, or for some subordinate partisan duty, yet he seems to have wanted that coolness, sagacity, and power of combination so essential in a commanding officer, and so imperatively required in a commander-in-chief. It is not surprising, therefore, that in that capacity, he should have acted only to ensure defeat and disgrace.

(36) Our author is not the only one who has blamed Gen. Putnam for the loss of Forts Montgomery and Clinton, and charged him with incapacity. It was a common report among those who were engaged in the defence of those forts, as well as among those who resided in the vicinity of them, that instead of attending to his duties as he should have done, he was intently engaged in a game of chess with a beautiful lady (said to be a daughter of Beverly Robinson, a noted tory), and that when warned of the threatened danger, he absolutely refused to leave the game, and did not do so until all hope of saving those posts had fled.

The following extracts, which we take from a work entitled "The Lives of Thomas, Knowlton, Scammel and Dearborn, by Charles Coffin," published in New York in 1845 [see pages 210–212], will show the opinion entertained of Gen. Putnam by some of the worthies of the Revolution who had the best opportunities of judging of his character:

"John Adams, in a letter to his wife, dated Baltimore, Feb. 21, 1777, says:

"I sincerely wish we could hear more from General Heath. Many persons are extremely dissatisfied with numbers of the general officers of the highest rank. I don't mean the Commander-in-Chief—his character is justly very high—but *Putnam, Spencer, and Heath, are thought by very few to be capable of the high commands they hold. We hear of none of their heroic deeds in arms. I wish they would all resign.*"

About the same time, Robert R. Livingston, then Chancellor of New York, in a letter to Washington, uses the following plain language:

"Your Excellency is not ignorant of the extent of Gen. Putnam's *capacity* and *diligence;* and how well soever they may qualify him for this important command [the Highlands], the prejudices to which his *imprudent levity to the disaffected, and too great intercourse with the enemy,* have given rise, have greatly injured his influence. How far the loss of Fort Montgomery and the subsequent ravages of the enemy are to be attributed to him, I will not venture to say, as this will necessarily be determined by a Court of Inquiry, whose determination I would not anticipate. Unfortunately for him, *the current of popular opinion in this and the neighboring States, and so far as I can learn, in the troops under his command, runs strongly against him.* For my own part, *I sincerely lament that his patriotism will not suffer him to take that repose to which his age and past services justly entitle him.*"

Governor Clinton also wrote pressingly to Washington requesting the removal of Putnam from the command in the Highlands.

In 1777, Congress appointed Governor Clinton a general officer in the army of the United States, and gave him the command on the North River, because, as President Hancock, in a letter to Clinton, says—"*an active and vigilant officer was required at that post.*" But Clinton's business as governor was so pressing, that he was compelled to decline the appointment, which continued Putnam in the command till March, 1778. In the latter part of 1777, after the surrender of Burgoyne's army, Washington was so desirous to be reinforced, in the vicinity of Philadelphia, by troops on the Hudson, under Gates and Putnam, that he sent Hamilton, his aid, to hasten their march, for his letters to them had not had the desired effect. Hamilton did not find either of those Generals disposed to comply with Washington's orders.

given through him. He addressed many letters to Washington on this subject, and in one, dated November 12, 1777, he says:

"By a letter of yesterday, Gen. Poor informs me he would certainly march this morning. I must do him the justice to say, he appears solicitous to join you, and that I believe the past delay is not owing to any fault of his, but is *wholly chargeable to Gen. Putnam.* Indeed, Sir, I owe it to the service to say, that every part *of this gentleman's conduct is marked with blunders and negligence and gives general disgust.*"

Again Hamilton says:

"*I doubt whether he will attend to anything I shall say, notwithstanding it comes in the shape of a positive order.*"

Col. Hamilton had the satisfaction of receiving a letter from Washington, of November 15, 1777, in which the Commander-in-Chief says:

"Dear Sir,—I have duly received your several favors from the time you left me to that of the 12th instant. I approve entirely of all the steps you have taken, and have only to wish that the *exertions of those you have had to deal with had kept pace with your zeal and good intentions.*"

Putnam's disobedience of the orders of Washington, which prevented the latter from even attempting the capture of Howe, which he had determined to effect, deeply affected Washington's mind: and we find in a letter dated Valley Forge, March 6, 1778, he thus expresses himself in reference to the command of Rhode Island:

"They also know with more certainty than I do, what will be the determination of Congress respecting Gen. Putnam; and of course whether the appointment of him to such a command as that at Rhode Island would fall within their views.

It being incumbent on me to observe, that *with such materials as I am furnished, the work must go on—whether well or ill is another matter. If, therefore, he and others are not laid aside, they must be placed where they can least injure the service.*"

In a letter of Washington to Putnam, dated Valley Forge, 16th March, 1778, he says:

"Gen. McDougall is to take command of the posts in the Highlands. My reason for making this change is owing to the *prejudices of the people, which whether well or ill grounded, must be indulged;* and I should think myself wanting in justice to the public and candor towards you, were I to continue you in a command, after I have been, almost in direct terms, informed that the *people of the State of New-York will not render the necessary support and assistance, while you remain at the head of that department.*"

See also *Sparks' Life and Writings of Washington*, vol. 5, pp. 280-284.

(19) The BEAR MARKET, or Hudson Market, as it had been previously called, was erected in the year 1771, and stood in Washington street, between Fulton and Vesey streets, near the water's edge. It derived the name of Bear Market from the circumstance that bear meat was the first kind of meat that was there exposed for sale. Upon its site, the present Washington Market was erected. This market was opened in the year 1813. The building is a spacious one, and is built of brick, and exclusively appropriated to the use of licensed butchers. At the ends of the wings and parallel to the front part, there is a wooden building for the accommodation of country people. Below this and close to the Hudson River

stands the Fish Market, which is likewise built of wood. The Washington market is chiefly patronized by the population of the southern and western parts of the city. The products of the North River country find their principal sale here.

(35) The OLD CITY HALL stood at the corner of Wall and Nassau streets, facing Broad street. It was constructed of the materials of a stone bastion in the line of the wall of defence along Wall street. After it was built, it is on record that it was "ordered that it be embellished with the arms of the King, and the Earl of Bellamont," which when done, the corporation ordered that the latter should be taken down and broken. The City Hall was erected in the year 1700, and was the proper prison of the city, having before it on Broad street, a whipping-post, pillory, etc. In the building were held the sessions of the Provincial Assembly, the Supreme Court, and the Mayor and Admiralty Courts. While the British held possession of the city, they used the City Hall as a guard-house for the main guard. There were dungeons below for the confinement of prisoners. At first only civil offenders were incarcerated there, but subsequently it became the place of imprisonment for whale-boatmen and robbers. During the latter part of the war the refugee clergymen preached in a court room on the second floor. While the building was occupied by the enemy, it was much injured by them, and they broke up and plundered the New York Society Library, then contained in one of the rooms. An eye-witness has affirmed that the soldiers were in the habit of carrying off the books in their knapsacks, and bartering them away for grog. After the Revolution, the building was fitted up under

the direction of the engineer, Major L'Enfant, for the reception of the first Federal Congress. It was here in the open gallery, in front of the Senate Chamber, in the view of an immense concourse of citizens collected on Broad street, that Washington took the oath of office as President of the United States, before Chancellor Livingston. The superb quarto Bible upon which the oath was taken, is still preserved by St. John's Lodge No. 1. Washington, on this occasion, was clad in a suit of brown cloth, of American manufacture—a steel-hilted sword by his side—his hair in a bag, and full powdered—silk hose and shoes with silver buckles. After the removal of Congress, the building was again occupied for city purposes, and continued to be thus used until the year 1813, when the "*Old Federal Hall*," as it had been latterly called, was demolished, and its site is now occupied by the fine marble building known as "*The Custom House*."

(39) JOHN SIMMONS was a noted tavern keeper in the city of New York. He carried on his business for many years in Wall, corner of Nassau street. It is believed that he had at one time the charge of the Old City Hall. He died about the year 1796. Mr. Simmons was a large, fleshy man, and on the day of his funeral, it was found necessary to cut away the street door of his house in order to let his coffin pass. Unlike most persons of obesity, he appears to have been of a petulant disposition, and is said to have been the terror of children, who would run when they saw him coming. He was well known to the urchins of his day by the irreverent cognomen of "*Old Simmons*." After his death, his widow conducted the business for some years.

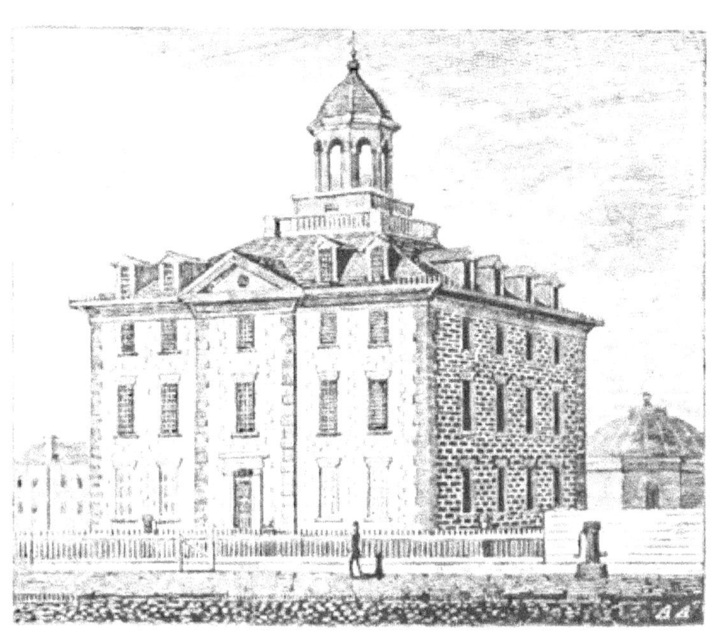

OLD PROVOST,

NEW YORK.

(10) The "New Jail," or the "*Provost*," as it was called in the Revolution, was a square, stone edifice, with a cupola, and was erected in 1758, in the Park, then known as the "Commons." Many interesting incidents are connected with the history of this building and its vicinity. Here Capt. afterwards Gen. McDougall was confined by the General Assembly, for what they called a libel; and here he was visited by the patriotic gentlemen and ladies who sympathized with him. When the British took possession of the city, they converted this building into a place of confinement for the "more notorious rebels, civil, naval and military. An admission into this modern bastile was enough to appal the stoutest heart. On the right of the main door was Capt. Cunningham's quarters; opposite to which was the guard-room, and within the first barricade was Sergeant O'Keefe's apartment. At the entrance door two sentinels were always posted, day and night. Two more were at the first and second barricades. These barricades were grated, barred and chained. Other sentinels were at the rear door, and on the platform at the grated door at the foot of the second flight of stairs, leading to the rooms and cells in the second and third stories. When a prisoner, escorted by soldiers, was led into the hall, the whole guard was paraded, and he was delivered over, with all formality, to Captain Cunningham or his deputy, and questioned as to his name, rank, size, age, etc., all of which were entered in a record-book. With the bristling of arms, unbolting of bars and locks, the clanking of enormous iron chains, and a vestibule as dark as Erebus, the unfortunate captive might well shrink under this infernal sight and parade of tyrannical power, as he crossed the threshold of that door which possibly closed on him for life. The northeast

chamber, turning to the left, on the second floor, was appropriated to officers and characters of superior rank and distinction, and was called 'Congress Hall.' So closely were the prisoners packed, that when they lay down at night to rest, when their bones ached on the hard oak planks, and they wished to turn, it was altogether by word of command—'*right—left*.' So wedged and compact were they, that they formed almost a solid mass of human bodies. In the daytime the packs and blankets of the prisoners were suspended around the walls, every precaution being used to keep the rooms ventilated, and the walls and floors clean, to prevent the jail fever. As the Provost was generally crowded with American prisoners, and British culprits of every description, it is really wonderful that infection never broke out within its walls. In this gloomy, terrific abode were incarcerated, at different periods, many American officers and citizens of distinction, awaiting with sickening hope and tantalizing expectation the protracted period of their exchange and liberation. Could those dumb walls speak, what scenes of anguish, what tales of agonizing woe might they not disclose. Among other characters who were there at the same time, were the famous Col. Ethan Allen, and Judge Fell, of Bergen County, New Jersey. When Capt. Cunningham entertained the young British officers accustomed to command the Provost guard, by dint of curtailing the prisoners' rations, exchanging good for bad provisions, and other embezzlements practiced, the captain, his deputy, and indeed the commissaries generally, were enabled to fare sumptuously. In the drunken orgies that usually terminated his dinners, the captain would order the rebel prisoners to turn out and parade for the amusement of his guests, pointing them out, "this is the damned rebel

Col. Ethan Allen—that a rebel Judge," etc. The treatment of the prisoners was as rigid as can be conceived. "They were closely confined in jail, without distinction of rank or character, amongst felons (a number of whom were under sentence of death), and their friends were not suffered to speak to them, even through the grates. They were compelled to subsist upon the scanty weekly allowance of two pounds of hard biscuit, and two pounds of raw pork per man, with no fuel to dress it. They were frequently supplied with water from a pump, where all kinds of filth that could render it obnoxious and unwholesome, was thrown (the effects of which were too often felt), and at the same time good water was as easily obtained. They were denied the benefit of a hospital, were not allowed to send for medicine, and no doctor permitted to visit them, even when they were in the greatest distress. Married men and others who lay at the point of death were refused the attendance of their wives or relatives, and those who attempted to gain admission were often beaten from the prison. Commissioned officers and other persons of character, without a cause were thrown into a loathsome dungeon, insulted in a gross manner, and vilely abused by a Provost marshal who was allowed to be one of the basest characters in the British army, and whose power was so unlimited that he caned an officer on a trivial occasion, and frequently beat the sick privates when unable to stand, many of whom were daily obliged to enlist in the New Corps, to prevent perishing for want of the necessaries of life. Neither pen, ink or paper was allowed—to prevent their treatment being made public—the consequence of which, the prisoners themselves dreaded, knowing the malignant disposition of their keeper." "It is said that Cunningham was only restrained from putting the prisoners to death, five or six of them of a night (back of the prison yard), by the distress of certain women in the neighborhood, who, pained by the cries for mercy which they heard, went to the Commander-in-chief, to whom they made the case known, and entreated him to discontinue the practice." After the Revolution the Provost was again used as a city jail, and was for some time the place of confinement for insolvent debtors, from which circumstance it obtained the name of the "Debtor's Prison." The building was subsequently altered for its present purpose, and is now known as the "*Hall of Records.*"

(11) SUSANNAH LEGGETT was the daughter of John Leggett, of West Farms, by his wife Sarah, and was born in Westchester County, N. Y., on the 23d day of July, 1758. She was married on the 3d day of February, 1779, to Abner Everitt, of Pennsylvania, who was by occupation a farmer. She died in Belvidere, N. J., on the 23d day of January, 1848, in the 90th year of her age. Her husband died in Pennsylvania on the 3d day of August, 1794, at the age of 40 years and six months. They had nine children, of whom there were four sons and five daughters. Abner Everitt was an officer in the army of the Revolution, and was at one time a prisoner with the enemy. There is a portrait of Mrs. Everitt, taken in her old age, and said to be an excellent likeness, in possession of her daughter, Mrs. John C. Van Allen, of this city.

(12) ANDREW NORWOOD was the husband of Mary Leggett, and brother-in-law to Major Leggett. Mr. Norwood was a shoemaker by trade. After the war he carried on the business at No. 12 Princess (now Beaver) street for many years.

(43) The surrender of Burgoyne and his army on the 17th of October, 1777, was by far the most fatal disaster which had occurred to the British in this country. While it gave for some time a death blow to their hopes of conquest, it inspired the Americans with a confidence to which many of them had heretofore been strangers. In every part of the country the news was considered important, but to the inhabitants of this city, which at that time consisted chiefly of British soldiers, sailors and royalists, the tidings must have been terrible indeed. It was now evident that the Americans had the ability to take care of themselves, and the consequence was, that they soon found friends who were not only able, but willing and ready to assist them.

(44) William Cunningham, the Provost-Marshal, used every precaution to keep the defeat of Burgoyne from the knowledge of his prisoners. He set a watch upon all persons visiting the Provost, that no communication of the fact might be made. A Miss Margaret Lent, who lived near the prison, and visited it frequently, with food, determined to inform the prisoners of our brilliant and cheering victory. She accordingly baked a letter containing the account in a *loaf of bread*. She carried it to the Provost, and directed that it should not be dispensed until she had time to reach her home. She was hardly across the threshold when a thundering shout from the prison announced to the keeper that the glorious achievement at Saratoga was no longer a secret. This intelligence, it is said, strengthened souls almost crushed by despair, for in it they saw glimmerings of our final triumph.

(45) CAPT. JAMES BREATH was born in the city of New York on the 7th October, 1771. He was married to Betsey,

eldest daughter of Major Leggett, on the 16th October, 1800. He was for many years captain of a merchant ship, sailing from New York to China. He afterwards left the sea, and went into the shipping business, in which occupation he remained for some time. In 1819, he moved to Marine Settlement, Illinois, where he died, October 26th, 1843. His wife, who was born at North Salem, N. Y., April 1st, 1778, died on the 12th February, 1859, in her 82d year, at the residence of her daughter in Danville, Kentucky. Capt. Breath had nine children, viz.:

JAMES SAUNDERS BREATH, born in New York, March 18, 1802.
ELIZABETH BREATH...... " " Jan. 9, 1804.
Died, Sept., 1820.
ABRAHAM BREATH....... " " Dec. 1, 1805.
EDWARD BREATH........ " " Jan. 22, 1808.
Died, Nov. 18, 1861.
JOHN BREATH........... " " Sept. 20, 1809.
Died, Nov. 27, 1863.
WM. LEGGETT BREATH... " " June 17, 1811.
REBECCA LEGGETT BREATH " " Nov. 15, 1813.
Died, Jan. 10, 1854.
MARY ADELINE BREATH.. " " Dec. 15, 1815.
SAMUEL M. BREATH...... " " Oct. 17, 1817.

(16) CATHARINE WILEY, who became the second wife of Major Leggett, was the daughter of an officer who was killed in the French war. She was born in the town of New Rochelle, Westchester County, N. Y., on the twenty-second day of July, in the year 1762. She was married to Major Leggett in New Rochelle, Jan. 3, 1784. She died in the

city of New York, on the twenty-ninth day of Nov., 1839. They had nine children, viz.:

1. Abraham Alsop Leggett, born in Charleston, S. C., Oct. 23, 1785.
2. Mary Norwood Leggett, born in Savannah, Ga., Aug. 1, 1788.
3. Sarah Wiley Leggett, born in Savannah, Ga., Aug. 23, 1790. Died, Nov. 30, 1791.
4. Sarah Leggett, born in Savannah, Ga., Dec. 15, 1792.
5. Louisa Leggett, born in Savannah, Ga., March 13, 1795. Died, April 20, 1820.
6. Jane Leggett, born in Savannah, Ga., July 26, 1797. Died, Aug. 10, 1865.
7. Wm. W. Leggett, born in Savannah, Ga., Nov. 15, 1799. Died, Feb. 11, 1800.
8. William Leggett (Editor, etc.), born in Savannah, Ga., April 30, 1801. Died, May 29, 1839.
9. Catharine Wiley Leggett, born in Savannah, Ga., March 19, 1804. Died, May 9, 1850.

(17) George Clinton was the youngest son of Col. Charles Clinton, and was born in Ulster, now Orange County, N. Y., on the 26th July, 1739. He studied law under William Smith, and soon rose to distinction. In 1775 he was a member of the Colonial Assembly, and in May of the same year, took his seat as a member of Congress. On the 25th March, 1777, he was appointed a Brigadier-General, and in April following, he became Governor of New York. On the advance of the British up the Hudson in October of that year, he took command of Fort Montgomery, where he and his brother James made a most gallant defence, and on being over-

powered by the enemy, he, with his brother, escaped under cover of the night. In the year 1801, he was again chosen Governor of New York, and in 1804, became Vice-President of the United States, which office he held at the time of his death. He was a man of great energy of character, and was possessed of most undaunted courage. He was distinguished as a soldier, a statesman and a patriot, and figures on the pages of history as one of the most illustrious characters of the revolution. He died at Washington, D. C., April 20th, 1812, in the 73d year of his age.

(48) FORT SLONGO was a strong military post at Treadwell's Neck, near Smithtown, Long Island. It was erected by a party of Tory wood-cutters, about one hundred and fifty in number, who committed many outrages and depredations. In the month of October, 1781, Major Benjamin Tallmadge attacked the fort, and destroyed it, carrying off a brass 3-pounder, the colors of the fort, seventy stand of arms, and a quantity of ammunition, besides taking a number of prisoners, and all without the loss of a man. He gives the following account of the expedition:

"The fortress at Treadwell's Neck, called Fort Slongo, seemed to demand attention, as the next in course to Fort St. George, which we had already taken. On the 1st of October, I moved my detachment of light infantry into the neighborhood of Norwalk. At the same time I directed a suitable number of boats to assemble at the mouth of the Saugatuck River, East of the town of Norwalk, and on the evening of the 2nd of October, 1781, at 9 o'clock, I embarked a part of my detachment, and placed Major Trescot at the head of it, with orders to assail the fort at a particular point.

The troops landed on Long Island by 4 o'clock, and at the dawn of day the attack was made and the fortress subdued. The blockhouse and other combustible materials were burnt, and the detachment and prisoners returned in safety."

Memoir of Col. Tallmadge, p. 46.

See also

Onderdonk's Suffolk and King's Counties, p. 105.

(19) TIMOTHY WILLIAMS was the son of Nathaniel Williams, a farmer of Huntington, L. I. His mother's maiden name was Rachel Fleet. She was the daughter of Thomas Fleet, of Huntington, who was by occupation a farmer. The subject of this note was born in Huntington, on the 25th day of December, 1756. He was in the army with Major Leggett during a considerable part of the war of the Revolution, and there was a most intimate and friendly relation between them. Mr. Williams followed the occupation of a merchant for many years after the war. He bore the reputation of a man of great integrity of character and amiability of disposition. He died in Huntington on the 26th day of August, 1811. His wife's maiden name was Jane Oakley. She was the daughter of Wilmot Oakley, a merchant of Sweet Hollow, L. I. She died in the city of New York on the 15th day of August, 1860, in the 90th year of her age. Mr. Williams had seven sons and three daughters. Of these, all are now living, except one daughter and two sons.

(20) The following account of this affair we take from one of the newspapers of the day:

"NEW-YORK, *October* 11.

Monday last were brought to town conducted by Captain Lake of the Loyal Refugees, and safely lodged in the

Provost of this city, the following rebel gentry, viz. Major Brush, Capt. Cornelius Conklin, Capt. J. Conklin, Capt. Rogers, and Lieutenant Faeley, all notorious offenders that have been long practiced in coming from the New England Shore to murder and plunder the King's loyal subjects on Long Island. They were last Saturday taken by Lieutenant Pendergrass and a party of Colonel Cuyler's Refugees, at Smith Town, with their whale boat and considerable booty. A certain Capt. Ketchum, one of the above gang, was killed in attempting to make his escape."

Gaine, Monday, Oct. 16, 1780.

www.ingramcontent.com/pod-product-compliance
Lightning Source LLC
Chambersburg PA
CBHW020328090426
42735CB00009B/1447